terms & conditions workbook

THE FINE PRINT TO AN ANTI-RACIST SOCIETY

Dr. Kiara Butler

WHITESIDE PUBLISHING

Whiteside Publishing is an independent publishing company that specializes in the production of Christian and self-help books.
Las Vegas, Nevada

terms & conditions by Kiara Butler
Senior Editor: Briana Whiteside
Published by Whiteside Publishing
Las Vegas, Nevada
For inquiries, please visit
www.brianawhiteside.com

Graphic Designer: EMBB Designs

CONTENTS

USER GUIDELINES

This workbook is your compass. Take as much time as you need with the reflection exercises and try to refrain from skipping ahead without doing the work required in the previous chapters. It is also important to familiarize yourself with the Terms & Conditions within each chapter before moving on to the next chapter.

CONDITIONS

Power: What Are You Willing to Lose?

Chapter 1 Reflection

Using the Terms provided for Chapter 1 on page 23, respond to the following reflection prompts in the space provided. When responding to the prompts, keep in mind that there is no correct or incorrect answer.

1. In what ways did you feel a personal connection to this chapter?

_____
_____
_____
_____
_____

2. How did this chapter push your thinking or cause you to question current beliefs?

_____
_____
_____
_____
_____
_____
_____
_____
_____
_____
_____
_____
_____
_____
_____
_____
_____

Personal Reflection

If you need to take a break at any point throughout your personal reflection, listen to your subconscious thoughts. Put a placeholder wherever you decide to take a moment and come back to the page when you are ready.

1. How does false charity work show up in your personal and/or professional life?

_____
_____
_____
_____
_____
_____
_____
_____

2. Describe an experience where you were in a position of power. How did being in this position make you feel?

_____
_____
_____
_____
_____
_____
_____
_____

3. How may your identities (race, gender, religion, sexual orientation, socio-economic status, etc.) influence the power you have? Is there a connection to your individual privilege?

_____
_____
_____
_____
_____
_____
_____
_____
_____
_____
_____
_____
_____
_____
_____
_____
_____
_____
_____
_____
_____
_____
_____
_____
_____
_____
_____
_____
_____
_____
_____

4. Describe an experience where you were powerless.
   How did being in this position make you feel?

5. In what ways can you use your power and privilege to benefit someone else?

6. Describe the social hierarchy in your own words. Where do you believe you fit within the hierarchy?

7. In what ways have you used your power and privilege for your benefit? Were there repercussions?

8. Why is the act of acknowledging your power and
   privilege important when creating an anti-racist
   society?

Personal Accountability

For every action there is a reaction. For every non-action, there is still a reaction but your willingness to take personal accountability may vary. It is easy to separate ourselves from a situation if we feel no connection to it. Let's create some action steps for intentionally shifting power dynamics within our personal lives, keeping in mind that these micro interactions will translate into societal changes on the macro level.

PERSONAL
Accountability

Changes You Plan to Make

List one or more best practices from the chapter that you plan to incorporate into your daily life.

- [ ]
- [ ]
- [ ]

Barriers

What barriers do you foresee in making this change?

- [ ]
- [ ]
- [ ]

Resources

What supports or resources need to be in place to overcome these barriers?

- [ ]
- [ ]
- [ ]

Shifts in Behavior

How do you plan to hold yourself accountable in making these shifts in behavior?

Empathy: Can Multiple Narratives Exist?

Chapter 2 Reflection

Using the Terms provided for Chapter 2 on page 46, respond to the reflection prompts in the space provided. When responding to the prompts, keep in mind that there is no correct or incorrect answer.

1. In what ways did you feel a personal connection to this chapter?

2. How did this chapter push your thinking or cause you to question current beliefs?

Personal Reflection

If you need to take a break at any point throughout your personal reflection, listen to your subconscious thoughts. Put a placeholder wherever you decide to take a moment and come back to the page when you are ready.

1. Describe an experience where you were the receiver of authentic empathy. How did it make you feel?

_____
_____
_____
_____
_____
_____
_____
_____
_____

2. Describe an experience where you were intentionally or unintentionally reluctant to express authentic empathy. What factors do you believe contributed to your reluctance? How may that experience impact how you receive others?

_____
_____
_____
_____
_____
_____
_____
_____
_____
_____
_____
_____
_____
_____
_____
_____

3. In what ways do you believe societal standards and stereotypes impact your ability to express authentic empathy?

4. How may your inability to express authentic empathy translate to how you show up in your relationships and public-facing spaces?

5. Have you ever felt that one or more of your core identities were invalidated or not received with authentic empathy? If so, list your core identities and explain why you believe this happened for each core identity. If not, list your core identities and explain why you believe this does not occur for each core identity.

6. Why is the act of expressing authentic empathy in your personal interactions critical when creating an anti-racist society?

Personal Accountability

For every action there is a reaction. For every non-action, there is still a reaction but your willingness to take personal accountability may vary. It is easy to separate ourselves from a situation if we feel no connection to it. Let's create some action steps for intentionally expressing authentic empathy within our personal lives, keeping in mind that these micro interactions will translate into societal changes on the macro level.

PERSONAL
Accountability

Changes You Plan to Make

List one or more changes you plan to make in your daily life to elevate marginalized populations.

- [ ]
- [ ]
- [ ]

Barriers

What barriers do you foresee in making this change?

- [ ]
- [ ]
- [ ]

Resources

What supports or resources need to be in place to overcome these barriers?

- [ ]
- [ ]
- [ ]

Shifts in Behavior

How do you plan to hold yourself accountable in making these shifts in behavior?

Relationships: Are You Really Well?

Chapter 3 Reflection

Using the Terms provided for Chapter 3 on page 62, respond to the following reflection prompts in the space provided. When responding to the prompts, keep in mind that there is no correct or incorrect answer.

1. In what ways did you feel a personal connection to this chapter?

_____

_____

_____

_____

_____

_____

_____

_____

_____

_____

_____

_____

_____

_____

_____

_____

2. How did this chapter push your thinking or cause you to question current beliefs?

_____
_____
_____
_____
_____
_____
_____
_____
_____
_____
_____
_____
_____
_____
_____
_____
_____
_____
_____

Personal Reflection

If you need to take a break at any point throughout your personal reflection, listen to your subconscious thoughts. Put a placeholder wherever you decide to take a moment and come back to the page when you are ready.

1. Describe a relationship in your life that fulfills your innate needs. Why does this relationship meet your needs? How does this relationship make you feel?

_____
_____

2. How do you know when you are genuinely connecting with others? In what ways do you ensure this connection?

3. Describe a relationship in your life that does not fulfill your innate needs. What is this relationship lacking? How does this relationship make you feel?

4. Do you work to establish genuine relationships with people who have core identities different from your own? If so, list out the reasons for establishing these relationships. If not, list out the reasons for reluctance.

5. Describe an experience where you felt excluded or did not belong? What were some of the indicators that made you feel this way?

6. How does patriarchy and/or toxic masculinity influence your ability to form genuine relationships?

7. Why is the act of establishing a sense of belonging important when creating an anti-racist society?

Personal Accountability

For every action there is a reaction. For every non-action, there is still a reaction but your willingness to take personal accountability may vary. It is easy to separate ourselves from a situation if we feel no connection to it. Let's create some action steps for intentionally establishing genuine relationships within our personal lives, keeping in mind that these micro interactions will translate into societal changes on the macro level.

PERSONAL
Accountability

Changes You Plan to Make

List one or more relationships you plan to strengthen in your personal and/or professional life.

- [ ]
- [ ]
- [ ]

Barriers

What barriers do you foresee in making this change?

- [ ]
- [ ]
- [ ]

Resources

What supports or resources need to be in place to overcome these barriers?

- [ ]
- [ ]
- [ ]

Shifts in Behavior

How do you plan to hold yourself accountable in making these shifts in behavior?

Mindset: At Whose Expense?

Chapter 4 Reflection

Using the Terms provided for Chapter 4 on page 78, respond to the following reflection prompts in the space provided. When responding to the prompts, keep in mind that there is no correct or incorrect answer.

1. In what ways did you feel a personal connection to this chapter?

_____
_____
_____

2. How did this chapter push your thinking or cause you to question current beliefs?

_____
_____
_____
_____
_____
_____
_____
_____
_____
_____
_____
_____
_____
_____
_____
_____
_____
_____

Personal Reflection

If you need to take a break at any point throughout your personal reflection, listen to your subconscious thoughts. Put a placeholder wherever you decide to take a moment and come back to the page when you are ready.

1. Describe a time when you were convinced you were right about something but then came to change your mind? What led to the change in your views?

2. How would you describe the American Dream? Do you believe there is an equitable chance for everyone to achieve it?

3. Have you ever had to consider your core identity (race, gender, religion, sexual orientation, socio-economic status, etc.) when navigating societal spaces? If so, describe your experience. If not, explain why you believe this isn't the case.

4. In what ways is your identity depicted within the United States? How does this viewpoint impact you?

5. What messages have you received from society about people with identities different from yours? How may those messages influence your perception of people with different identities?

6. In what ways have you contributed to societal
   standards of appropriateness (keeping in mind that
   we all contribute to varying systems of oppression)?

7. In what ways have you contributed to the amplification of the dominant white narrative in your personal and/or professional life?

8. Why is the act of gaining self-awareness and ongoing reflection necessary when creating an anti-racist society?

Personal Accountability

For every action there is a reaction. For every non-action, there is still a reaction but your willingness to take personal accountability may vary. It is easy to separate ourselves from a situation if we feel no connection to it. Let's create some action steps for intentionally gaining self-awareness through ongoing reflection, keeping in mind that these micro interactions will translate into societal changes on the macro level.

P E R S O N A L
Accountability

Changes You Plan to Make

List one or more changes you plan to make in your daily life to expand your cultural knowledge.

- [ ]
- [ ]
- [ ]

Barriers

What barriers do you foresee in making this change?

- [ ]
- [ ]
- [ ]

Resources

What supports or resources need to be in place to overcome these barriers?

- [ ]
- [ ]
- [ ]

Shifts in Behavior

How do you plan to hold yourself accountable in making these shifts in behavior?

TERMS OF USE

In each chapter, you were tasked with listing one or more changes you plan to make in your daily life. Using the space provided below, create personal accountability measures by identifying: 1.) the specific action; 2.) how you will measure the change over time; 3.) the resources you will need; 4.) the importance of this change in creating an anti-racist society; and 5.) the date you will begin incorporating this action into your day-to-day life.

S M A R T

SPECIFIC   MEASUREABLE   ATTAINABLE   RELEVANT   TIMELY

About the Author

Dr. Kiara Butler is a social entrepreneur, keynote speaker, and Founder of Diversity Talks. She is a strong advocate for youth voice, and in her current work she focuses on bringing the voices of marginalized groups to the forefront. Because of her advocacy, she has been recognized for her work in various capacities, such as Forbes 30 Under 30, TEDxProvidence, PBS, EdSurge, The Boston Globe, and The Providence Journal.

Made in the USA
Monee, IL
06 June 2023

35351199R00031